D0995646

How To Save A Life

How To Save A Life

Becoming a Christian

Krish Kandiah

Authentic

MILTON KEYNES ● COLORADO SPRINGS ● HYDERABAD

15 14 13 12 11 10 09   7 6 5 4 3 2 1

First published 2009 by Authentic Media
9 Holdom Avenue, Bletchley, Milton Keynes, Bucks, MK1 1QR, UK
1820 Jet Stream Drive, Colorado Springs, CO 80921, USA
Medchal Road, Jeedimetla Village, Secunderabad 500 055, A.P., India
www.authenticmedia.co.uk
Authentic Media is a division of IBS-STL U.K., limited by guarantee,
with its Registered Office at Kingstown Broadway, Carlisle, Cumbria
CA3 0HA. Registered in England & Wales No. 1216232. Registered
charity 270162

British Library Cataloguing in Publication Data
A catalogue record for this book is available from the British Library

ISBN-13: 978-1-85078-821-8

Cover Design by David McNeill
Print Management by Adare Carwin
Printed and bound in Great Britain by J.H. Haynes & Co., Sparkford

To Joel, Luke, Anna and Emily

Contents

To save a life

Minutes to midnight, and Tamaz, as usual, had not saved a life all day. He was just an ordinary English Literature student trying to survive university under difficult circumstances. This week he had been looking after a foreign exchange student: showing him the sights of Tbilisi, pointing out the landmarks and explaining their history and significance. As Tamaz walked his guest home that warm night the café terraces were still crowded as people chatted and chilled under the stars, enjoying the coffee and the Georgian atmosphere. But Tamaz had no time to indulge in that tonight. It had been a busy day and they needed to get home to sleep.

Without warning, the atmosphere was suddenly shattered as a gunman opened fire. In a flash, Tamaz jumped towards his guest, who was absent-mindedly looking up at the sky as though expecting to see fireworks. Tamaz grabbed his T-shirt and shouted at him to run. Another round of fire and Tamaz pulled him to the ground briefly before they tried once again to run for their lives. The street was in total chaos as bullets ripped through the air. The crowd scattered in every direction and the shots continued. Perhaps it would have been better for Tamaz to lead the way. After all, the visitor had no idea where he was going. But Tamaz stayed behind him, deliberately blocking the line of fire and protecting his new friend.

Seconds later, after what had seemed an age, Tamaz finally managed to push his friend around a corner, out of harm's way. However, as he dived after him a bullet hit him from behind and he shouted out in agony. Tamaz spent most of that night in the hospital with his visitor friend at his side, and during the long hours of waiting, a story was pieced together of a laughing policeman who had had too much to drink and had spewed gunfire indiscriminately on a busy street before passing out.

Tamaz saved my life that day. Within a microsecond of hearing the first shot, he decided to go way beyond what was expected of him as my guide and trade his own welfare for mine. Five minutes earlier, and I didn't even know my life would need saving. Five minutes later, and my host became my hero.

Five years earlier, my life was saved by someone else. Someone else who had seen the danger I was in way before I did; someone else who had put my welfare above his own; someone else who had cried out in agony in my place; someone else who went from being a perfect stranger to a lifelong friend.

This second story is not unique to me. Millions of people through the centuries and around the world have gladly committed their lives to following Jesus because of what he did to save them. Every day Jesus saves lives, and this book aims to explain in a straightforward way how you too can be saved.

Perhaps I should mention at this point that all you need for Jesus to save your life is to say a simple prayer such as

> Lord God,
> Forgive me for what I have done.
> Thank you for what Jesus did for me
>   on the cross.
> I want to live for you.
> Amen.

However, these few short words require serious consideration and serious commitment. In that sense, they are like the 'I do' in a marriage ceremony, said after months of preparation. You may already feel that you can say this prayer and mean it. Or you may feel that you can't say these words – perhaps you feel you are too good or too bad for it, or that it's too late or too soon, for this decision.

Maybe becoming a Christian seems as foreign to you as a day out in Tbilisi. This book will be your guide, pointing out the key landmarks to starting a relationship with God. But be warned, you may find that your life needs saving on the way. Read on to find out what Jesus did for you, if you could say this prayer and really mean it and what difference it would make to your life.

The prayer is adapted from the final words of a man who died on the cross next to Jesus: the last life Jesus saved before he died. Here is his story, according to Jesus' biographer, Luke.

Two other men, both criminals, were also led out with him to be executed. When they came to the place called the Skull, there they crucified him, along with the criminals—one on his right, the other on his left. Jesus said, "Father, forgive them, for they do not know what they are doing." And they divided up his clothes by casting lots.

The people stood watching, and the rulers even sneered at him. They said, "He saved others; let him save himself if he is the Christ of God, the Chosen One."

The soldiers also came up and mocked him. They offered him wine vinegar and said, "If you are the king of the Jews, save yourself."

There was a written notice above him, which read: THIS IS THE KING OF THE JEWS.

One of the criminals who hung there hurled insults at him: "Aren't you the Christ? Save yourself and us!"

But the other criminal rebuked him. "Don't you fear God," he said, "since you are under the same sentence? We are punished justly, for we are getting what our deeds deserve. But this man has done nothing wrong."

Then he said, "Jesus, remember me when you come into your kingdom."

Jesus answered him, "I tell you the truth, today you will be with me in paradise."

Maybe becoming a Christian seems as foreign to you as a day out in Tbilisi. **This book will be your guide.**

When an unknown author from Edinburgh discovered that her first children's novel had been rejected by publishers Penguin, she was gutted. But not half as gutted as the Penguin commissioning editor was when the first story about a young boy in foster care who is accepted into wizard school unleashed the worldwide Harry Potter phenomenon.

When an unknown band played a sign-up gig for Decca Records on 1 January 1962, they were devastated to be told 'guitar groups are on the way out' and turned down for a contract. But not half as devastated as Decca, when Beatlemania went on, with EMI's support, to take the planet by storm.

When an unknown carpenter's son, from the middle of nowhere, claimed to be God himself, he was executed on a cross for treason. But that attempt to silence Jesus of Nazareth turned into the single most significant and talked-about event in human history.

Jesus has been dismissed by many people over the last two thousand years as merely a great religious teacher who experienced an unfortunate miscarriage of justice. But if, as J.K. Rowling and Paul McCartney might tell us, it is possible to stare a mind-blowing discovery in the face and completely miss its significance, then it may be worth taking a closer look. It is possible we might discover that we are in more trouble than we ever realized and that our life is more precious than we ever imagined.

The account of the crucifixion in Luke's biography of Jesus shows us that many of our first-century counterparts, good, bad and ugly, dismissed the whole event as a joke. But one person saw something different that saved his life.

The GOOD

We are used to hearing public figures ridicule the Christian faith. Some prominent scientists, popular radio presenters and high-profile authors seem to gain a kind of perverse pleasure from openly deriding all things Christian. So we should not be surprised to discover in Luke's account that educated and powerful social figures – the Jewish rulers – were sneering at Jesus even in his hour of death.

What is surprising is that the rulers were to pitting themselves against the religious leaders – they were the religious leaders. They believed they were good at being good, and good at guarding the good in society. They lived the good life, so when Jesus came along, they saw him as a threatening young radical who had dared to question their rights and their rituals. By criticizing their double standards and undermining their power base, Jesus made enemies of the great and the good in Jewish religious society.

Jesus challenged the religious leaders for their hypocrisy. Outwardly they were fine upstanding people, but Jesus saw through this and spoke openly about how they were going through the religious motions, dishing out lots of rules, yet inwardly ignoring God and not lifting a finger to help the needy people around them. Jesus likened them in Luke 11:44 to unmarked graves: a serene picture of lush grass and spring flowers at one level, whilst below the surface lay repulsive rotting corpses. They looked good, but internally their motives were rotten to the core.

Many people would be surprised to find themselves agreeing with Jesus here. The hypocrisy of religion is not attractive. In the name of religion wars have been waged, ethnic cleansing has taken place and child abuse has been covered up. Atheism has also been used as an excuse to carry out all sorts of atrocities: the root of these problems is the human capacity for evil. Jesus has no time for empty religion, for the thin veneer of turning up to religious services, wearing the right clothes, and reading the right books when underneath there are hidden motives, self-serving agendas, and cold rotten hearts. He wants to get to the heart of the issue.

So Jesus was no friend of religion – not if religion meant using God's name as an excuse to exploit people and initiate regulations or as a mascot for nationalistic pride. Jesus was no friend of the religious – he did not spend all his time in the temple or with the good, the rich and the famous, but in the homes of the underclass of society.

He ate and drank with politically unacceptable Roman collaborators, morally unacceptable prostitutes, physically unacceptable lepers and ethnically unacceptable Samaritans. Jesus welcomed their friendship and hospitality and showed them unconditional respect and compassion.

Jesus taught that becoming a Christian was not about becoming religious, nor conforming to an empty set of rituals and regulations, but becoming like him. This teaching and lifestyle were simply too inconvenient for the religious leaders who were watching. They could not stand him. So they bribed one of Jesus' friends to ambush him, had him abducted in the middle of the night and then questioned him until they could land him with something incriminating, so they could drag him to the Roman authorities to request the death penalty. Their plan worked. The rulers succeeded in having the whistleblower sent to his death and now they took their moment to gloat.

Jesus' teaching is still unacceptable to many people today. For those of us who manage to appear 'good', it is extremely uncomfortable to have the purity of Jesus' life and teaching challenge us to a new standard inside and out. Sometimes it feels more convenient to do away with Jesus altogether, by living without reference to him or by domesticating him into just another good man with some handy tips for being an upright member of society.

We must hear the warning of the actions of the 'good' religious rulers, who rather than face up to the truth of their hypocrisy, sought to silence Jesus through murder. We must be careful not to follow their example and reject Jesus without checking whether what he says is true, however uncomfortable that may be.

The BAD

The Roman soldiers were the first-century villains and were very good at being very bad. They enjoyed all the privileges of an occupying force at the expense of everybody else, whether by forcing hiked-up taxes on the people, or making passers-by carry their luggage. They reinforced their position by publicly humiliating anyone who stood against their power. Crucifixions were a highly public way of reminding the people the Romans were in charge. Crosses with dying criminals and political revolutionaries on them were put up by the side of roads or in public spaces as government health warnings: 'Challenging the Romans is dangerous to your health.'

It is little wonder that the soldiers attending Jesus' crucifixion decided to add insult to injury. They took the opportunity to publicly mock him in his final few hours, as well as gamble for his clothes while he was still breathing. Their governor, Pontius Pilate, also saw the crucifixion as an opportunity for political propaganda: he used the cross as a macabre living signpost to the futility of standing against the might of Rome by posting a sign on it with the derisive strapline, 'Jesus Christ, King of the Jews'.

The powerful Romans mocked Jesus' claim to be king. After all, he had never raised an army nor lifted a sword in battle; he was just an insignificant carpenter's son from a tiny backwater of the vast and invincible Roman Empire with a claim that seemed too big for his sandals. The Romans were not looking for a new king, especially one who was starting a revolution of peace. To them, Jesus was just a joke.

I can empathize a little with the Romans' position on account of me being a terrible passenger. I am constantly trying to put the brakes on, watch the speedometer and lean over to get a look-in on the rearview mirror whilst offering unwanted advice to the driver, warning about hazards ahead, and grabbing the door handle in nervous panic. I want to be in control. I like driving where I want, how I want and at the speed I want. The Romans are just like me and others: we don't like to have our fingers prized off the steering wheel.

Most of us are not looking for a new king either and we feel particularly nervous about someone who could steer our lives in a totally new direction. We like to feel we are good at being in control of our lives and feel threatened by Jesus' claim to be king of the world. It is simpler to dismiss him as a joke.

We must hear the warning of the Roman soldiers. They may have felt they were part of the mighty Roman Empire, but in the grand scheme of things, Jesus has had more lasting influence on history. The Colosseum is in ruins, and

Caesars are relegated to the pages of history books or glass cabinets of museums. Jesus, on the other hand, continues to have profound influence on society and even today over two billion people on the planet claim to know him personally and follow him no matter what. It would seem the joke backfired.

The UGLY

The good people felt they were too good for Jesus. Even the bad people felt they were too good for Jesus. The third group of people in the account is the 'ugly' people: two convicted criminals, the worst of Israel's lawbreakers, also on death row. Nobody liked them, and nobody was going to mourn their deaths.

Here were two men who had lived similar lives of crime and were dying similar deaths of shame. Externally, they were probably difficult to tell apart. But internally, they were very different. The first one uses his last breaths to hurl insults at Jesus along with the religious rulers and the Roman soldiers. The other uses his last breaths to sort his life out when he sees something nobody else sees. (To distinguish between them, we will refer to the first convict as the criminal, and the second as the thief.)

The criminal taunts Jesus, 'Save yourself and us', as though challenging Jesus would persuade him to get the criminal off the hook or at least off the cross. But when he realizes Jesus has no intention of staging an eleventh-hour Houdini-style escape and Marx-style revolution, he shouts it only to humiliate the disappointing man next door.

Many of us can relate to this criminal. We would like Jesus to deliver something, but when he doesn't, we dismiss him as a disappointment. Perhaps we have prayed for sick or dying friends or relatives. Perhaps we have expected him to do something about the unfairness of the world around us, local or global. Perhaps we have hoped that he would do something miraculous just for us. And when we haven't seen any dramatic intervention, we wonder if he is even there at all. The irony is that as the criminal taunted 'Save yourself and us' as though Jesus was incapable of saving anybody, Jesus was 'saving' millions of people, not by rescuing them from the cross, but by rescuing them through the cross. We will come back to this vital distinction later.

Some people say they have no time for Jesus in this world, although they admit they may change their mind on their deathbeds, as an insurance policy for whatever is to come next. But this criminal's reaction to Jesus is a stark warning to those of that mentality. Even at his death, he sees fit only to throw blame and insults. He is like a man who walks into a house and thinks he can smell gas. It briefly crosses his mind to call the gas company, but then as he wanders around the house sniffing the air for a while the smell seems to lessen and disappear altogether. But the gas has not gone away: the man has just become acclimatized to the smell. Instead of calling for help as he originally intended, he passes out from the fumes. Perhaps this criminal missed out on calling out to Jesus for help because he had become so used to ignoring the voice of his conscience – so much so that even when he was staring death in the face he couldn't hear it anymore. Perhaps this man was so acclimatized to getting what he wanted the way he wanted it that even pain and imminent death could not change his perspective.

It seems crazy that a man dying on a cross would expend his failing energy on mocking the only person who could possibly save him. But many of us are equally short-sighted as we ignore our consciences drawing us towards God, instead presenting him with an ultimatum that he live up to our demands. If we continue in this way, we run the risk of the same fate as the man who died next to the Saviour of the world without being saved.

An unlikely exception

I love the Hans Christian Andersen story of the emperor and his new clothes. I love hearing how the rich and powerful king is duped by the smooth-talking tailors from out of town. I love how they talk him into wearing invisible clothes while thinking it is the finest cloth that only the truly discerning can see. I love hearing how the ministers are far too afraid to speak up, and would rather keep the king happy with lies, even if that means allowing him to process through the town in his birthday suit. I love imagining how the crowd can't believe their eyes that their king is parading stark naked in front of them. I love it when the sole voice of an innocent child speaks out the blindingly obvious truth.

The story reminds me of Luke's account of another naked king, this time not one who was duped but one who was dismissed. Against the roar of the crowd, against the blinkered opinion of the educated and against the wishful thinking of the powerful, a sole voice speaks out the blindingly obvious truth: 'Don't you fear God?'

Everyone else witnessing the crucifixion that day seems to be enjoying the chance to gloat. Whether the good, the bad or the ugly, they all think they are better than Jesus. The religious leaders, the Roman soldiers and the dying criminal all measured Jesus against their own personal agendas. And Jesus fell short: he was the wrong kind of messiah for the Jewish authorities; the wrong kind of king for the Romans; and the wrong kind of saviour for a crooked criminal. All of them mock Jesus – except for one man. The thief dying next to Jesus decides to break away from the majority as he realizes he is about to meet God.

We need to take his question seriously: 'Don't you fear God?' It reveals four things the thief realized in the light of his imminent death. Firstly, he believed God existed; secondly, he believed he would meet him when he died; thirdly, he believed Jesus represented God; and fourthly, he believed he would be held to account for his actions in this life. His question set him apart from the crowd: fearing instead of jeering.

What was it about this thief that he came to such a radically different conclusion about Jesus? Most of us, like the religious, the powerful, the crowds and the criminal measure Jesus up against our own standards and find that he falls short: he is just not good enough for us. Some of us, like the thief, measure ourselves up against Jesus and realize that Jesus is far too good for us and we fall short. Perhaps in the face of this we need to be prepared to acknowledge the possibility of God's existence and his status, and perhaps we need to be prepared to meet him when we die.

> 'Don't you fear God since you are under the same sentence?'

The first words of our prayer to become a Christian state that we acknowledge, like the thief on the cross, that God is there and is to be feared and honoured. Out of respect, we address him 'Lord God'. This is not an easy thing to say: we are so used to being masters of our own lives. But it is a necessary start for anyone who knows they are not good enough and wants God to save their life.

2: 'I'm too bad . . .'

I thought I was good at volleyball. I was captain of my sixth-form squad, and even though we were just a comprehensive school, we crushed our local rivals: the team from the exclusive public school up the road. Admittedly, they were an all-girl team and at least three years younger than us. But it was a hard-earned victory, nonetheless. I thought I was good at volleyball so I strutted confidently into the team selection meeting of the University volleyball club. I stood there boldly as the other players lined up. I became slightly unnerved when I saw the net we were using was pulled taut, and elevated beyond what I was used to. I began to feel a little uneasy when I noticed that most of the players were peering down at me from high altitude. I became exceedingly uncomfortable when the first guy stepped forward to serve and seemed to be doing some kind of karate move on the ball that I had never seen before, instantaneously teleporting it from one side of the court to the other.

I did make it onto the University volleyball team – it was my job to bring the oranges around at half-time and to lob drinks up to the seven-foot-tall first-team players when they got thirsty! I thought I was good at volleyball until I met people who were actually really good at volleyball.

In the last chapter we saw that many people think they are good. We compare ourselves with the people around us and easily spot their flaws. We even scour the tabloids to make sure we compare favorably to the celebrities who flaunt their got-it-all lifestyles. When we hear that another fairytale marriage has broken up, or another star is struggling with drug addiction, or another household name has been arrested for speeding, we feel better about ourselves. **We like to think we are good at being good.**

I thought I was good at being good. I paid my bus fares, never joined in the bullying at school and respected my parents' wishes, at least most of the time, which seemed to be good enough to beat most people I knew.

Then I met Jesus. I began to read in the Bible the remarkable story of this man who had grown up in an inconsequential town, apprenticed in a local small-time business. Then he had jacked it all in to become a traveller and freelance teacher with twelve mismatched volunteer students. That was all well and good, but as I read more I became unnerved as he taught standards that were even higher than the volleyball net I couldn't reach. I began to feel a little uneasy as he showed what compassion and kindness really looked like. I became exceedingly uncomfortable as he started to expose the real hypocrisies inside people's hearts. I thought I was good at being good until I met Jesus: the Jesus who not only taught about another kingdom and gave people a taste of it with his miraculous healings, but also showed how to live life perfectly.

This is what the thief saw, and with this perspective, he looked at Jesus and said to the other criminal: 'We are getting what our deeds deserve. But this man has done nothing wrong.'

When he recognized he was accountable to God for his life, and he measured himself against the perfect standards set by the life and teachings of Jesus, the thief knew that his life and Jesus' life were worlds apart.

'We are getting what our deeds deserve. But this man has done nothing wrong.'

I didn't last long on the University volleyball team. I brought the oranges and water bottles for a while, but each time I went I felt smaller and smaller. I started to make excuses to miss the training times and gradually I stopped going altogether. I did have a busy course and other activities I wanted to pursue, but the real reason I walked away was because I couldn't face being the worst (last-resort substitute) volleyball player on the squad.

Many people have a similar experience when they begin to get to know Jesus. Thinking about Jesus' goodness can be as painful as trying to stare directly into the sun. Our eyes are not equipped for the brilliance and our retinas are quickly damaged by the intense light. Reading about the quality of Jesus' life can burn our consciences. When we see just how high his standards are and how far short we fall, we begin to avoid him altogether, just as we avoid staring at the sun, or as I avoided my volleyball practices. But there are three good reasons why there is no reason to walk away in embarrassment from Jesus' purity. In Jesus we find the compassion of God, the forgiveness of God and the justice of God – the three things we need for Jesus to save our life.

1. Compassion

The iceberg has been struck, the liner is taking on water and the lifeboats are being deployed. Ruth DeWitt Bukater in James Cameron's movie *Titanic* is being helped into a lifeboat when she asks a ridiculous question: if the lifeboats are first class. Although thousands of lives including her own are in imminent mortal danger, all she can think about is not mixing with the riff-raff.

Some people spend their whole lives protecting and showing off their superior status. Their lives become a living advertisement to themselves as they define themselves by what they drive, which label they wear, what they do or who they know, as well as who they do not. If anyone had cause for a superiority complex it was Jesus. He was God in human form. He had power beyond imagination, utter moral purity, as well as infinite wisdom, status and knowledge.

But Jesus did not flaunt any of that. He did not use his high standards and status to make others feel like second-class citizens. Nobody was too bad for Jesus. Compassion was Jesus' trademark and people others rejected he would draw close and offer them hope and dignity.

If anyone feels too bad for Jesus, they only need to take a look at this thief. He had probably lived a life of crime with little regret. He had no doubt caused a lot of grief to a lot of people, and many of the onlookers would have felt only too glad justice was being served as he faced torture and death. There was no way he could begin to justify his career choice, defend his actions or excuse his punishment. Yet Jesus, in the agony of the cross is not too self-absorbed to reach out even to him. He is compassionate to the end.

Many people imagine Jesus is watching them like an angry headmaster: standing at a distance, tut-tutting, pointing the finger and making a note of every infringement, as he gets ready to tell them off and throw them into eternal detention. But this is a million miles away from the picture the Bible paints of Jesus. One story Jesus told to help us is of a loving father whose wilful child has run off with the family savings and disowned him. We can easily visualize what a teenager with more money than sense would do, and when the cash, friends and luck run out, he ends up destitute, willing to do anything just to survive. The boy decides as a last resort to beg his dad to bail him out and he sets off home expecting what he deserves: a closed door and an angry father. But even from a far distance his dad spots him and runs to him, arms open wide and tears in his eyes. Jesus says this is the way God feels about us. God's heart is one of compassion, and if we turn to him we will discover his welcome and his warm embrace.

Jesus is morally perfect, but he is not distant. When the thief looked at Jesus, he saw him as a man right alongside him suffering the exact same pain. Jesus knows what we go through when we struggle and suffer, and he always comes alongside with open arms, not wanting anyone to avoid him, no matter how totally we have failed.

2. Forgiveness

Picture another father–son scene as my seven year old and I happily cycle home from a cross-country bike ride singing manly cycling songs together and enjoying each other's company. As we approach the cul-de-sac where we live, my son, who usually puts his bike straight in the garage, decides to try out a stunt. Before I can stop him the bike slips right into the side of my neighbour's brand new car. I cringe at the noise which sounds like fingernails scratching a blackboard. And where there was once unblemished glistening silver paintwork, there is now a long ugly gash of exposed metal.

I was cross. In my head, I pictured Homer Simpson throttling his son Bart. And I knew what else Homer would do. He would tell his son to act innocent and avoid his neighbour for a few months. My son and I had a heated discussion about why we should not be in this position. That didn't help. Eventually, we agreed on something. Together we went over to the neighbour's house and my son owned up and apologized and I offered to pay the cost of repairing the damage.

Often we try to get through life by avoiding the people we hurt. We try the same technique with God. We hope by keeping our heads low we won't have to face the consequences of our actions. So we live with guilty consciences and the fear that sooner or later we will have to face God. The thief knew time had run out for him. He could no longer kid himself he would not be held accountable. It was time for him to own up and ask for forgiveness, but who was going to pay for the damage?

3. Justice

Admirers of Princess Diana don't wear smashed Mercedes cars on gold chains around their necks. Moslems don't celebrate the poisoning that led to Mohammed's death. Fans of Kurt Cobain don't put up posters of shotguns on their walls. But Christians persist in using the cross on necklaces, greetings cards and churches, and devote the Easter celebration to the memory of the barbaric way in which Jesus was tortured and executed.

The cross is unashamedly the central symbol of the Christian faith, and it is precisely the place where Jesus died that we find out the mechanics of how Jesus can save a life. It is on the cross that the damage is paid for the scrapes into which we have got ourselves, and accounts are settled.

To understand this, we need to see the whole of history not from our default perspective, but from God's perspective. Christians believe God created the universe for us to cultivate and enjoy, and when we launched a *coup d'état* and commandeered the planet for our own ends, he didn't scrap it and start again but came up with a long-term rescue plan.

God initially set up a system of animal sacrifices to demonstrate that the consequence of rebellion was death; whereby a sheep killed could represent a person who messed up, and the books would be balanced. So for centuries the people of God kept sinning and sacrificing and sinning and sacrificing. It was a laborious system, but it was only ever meant to be temporary. Hundreds of years before Jesus was born in Bethlehem, one of God's messengers glimpsed God's ultimate means of settling the account.

> But he was pierced for our transgressions,
>   he was crushed for our iniquities;
>   the punishment that brought us peace was
>   upon him,
>   and by his wounds we are healed.
> We all, like sheep, have gone astray,
>   each of us has turned to his own way;
>   and the LORD has laid on him
>   the iniquity of us all.

(Isaiah 53:5–6)

'Transgressions', 'iniquities' and 'going our own way' are strong words to ram home the fact that from God's perspective each of us has fallen far short of the standard expected. If we are uncomfortable with the word sin, we will now be really squirming in our seats. But instead of asking for a sheep to trade places with a person, the prophet announces that God is going to allow a person to trade places with all of us wayward lost sheep. This person would be pierced, crushed and punished by God so we all could be healed and forgiven. This settling of accounts was going to be a worldwide colossal event involving the violent torturous death of God's chosen one.

This is the path Jesus willingly chose to travel. It is a vivid picture of the cross hundreds of years before it happened. From God's perspective, this event marked the pivotal point of human history, the place where accounts could be settled once and for all.

The cross is so central to Christianity and yet many of us miss its point. Some people believe the cross of Jesus was simply a wonderful grand gesture of love. If I had thrown myself into the Pacific Ocean on my honeymoon and drowned as an act of love, my new wife would hardly have been bowled over by my show of affection. A bunch of flowers would have been a much better bet. This theory simply doesn't hold water – dying does not in itself communicate love. However, imagine I had seen the dorsal fin of a great white headed straight for my bride, and dived in to wrestle the deadly shark, thereby buying her time to reach safety, despite being devoured by it myself. Now my death would be an indication of the depth of my love for her because I was willing to sacrifice my own life in her place. This is precisely what Jesus' death was about – a demonstration of love because he saved our lives, taking our place before the righteous anger of God the Father at our sin, enabling us to go free.

Crime and punishment, pardon and peace

The thief on the cross and Jesus traded places that day. His crimes needed to be punished and paid for, but they were transferred onto Jesus. While the other criminal was shouting 'Save yourself and us', Jesus was refusing to save himself so that we could be saved, not from physical death, but from God's punishment. We are pardoned, and, therefore, at peace with God because Jesus was punished in our place for our crimes.

Not long ago a highly unusual listing came up on eBay. 'New life for sale' offered Nicael Holt, a twenty-four-year-old Australian philosophy student. Open to the highest bidder, Mr Holt was willing to sell his name, all of his possessions, and his phone number. He even promised his 'cranky girlfriend', fifteen friends and two enemies. He was only withholding his passport, inheritance rights and academic qualifications from the lucky bidder. Someone eventually paid 7500 Australian dollars (around 3500 pounds) for Nicael Holt's life.

I wonder if he felt disappointed that was all he was worth. When Jesus offers 'New life for sale' there is no cost to us. But the cost to God was the king's ransom of Jesus' life that was paid to buy our forgiveness. The cross of Jesus tells us peace between us and God is worth much more to God than a few thousand pounds.

When my son apologized to our neighbour for scratching his car with his bicycle stunt and heard the words 'It's OK, all is forgiven and sorted,' he was able to feel relieved in a way that he never would have if I had just said, 'Never mind – let's pretend it wasn't you.' We walked together into the house, and he turned to me to say sorry. He knew he had let me down, made me cross and caused me to fork out for the damage. When I offered him forgiveness, and told him I loved him anyway, we became closer than any bike ride could have brought us. It was a precious moment.

God delights in forgiving sinful people. As is so often true in life, forgiveness and peace can only come after we have owned up to our failings. Our failure to live up to Jesus' standards is not just a minor slip-up: it is part of a bigger picture of our rebellion against God. We live as if God is an irrelevance, we ignore everything to do with him and we pursue our own pleasures and stunts. Often, it takes a tragedy or crisis to make us face up to the truth that we have let God down. But the amazing thing about God is he is not too proud to accept us even when our apology comes when we have run out of our resources, only after all the things we were chasing failed to satisfy us. God does not gloat or preach or say 'I told you so.' Nor does he brush us aside and say 'Never mind'. He offers the only way forward: he offers forgiveness at the highest price possible to him, a settling of accounts at no cost to ourselves and an intimate relationship to anyone however bad, who recognizes their sin and is prepared to say the second line of our prayer: 'Forgive me for what I have done.'

Often, it takes a **tragedy** or crisis to make us face up to the **truth** that we have let God down.

3: 'It's too late . . .'

My heart was beating fast. It was a dark road, the rain was pelting down and someone was trying to cut me up on the bend. But I was having none of it. I pressed the accelerator and gained an advantage. I felt the car going into a power slide as it travelled sideways round the corner. I couldn't hold it, and as I watched the vehicle overtake me, my own wheels were off the road hurtling over the grass. I could hear my son's voice shouting 'No!' behind me. I braked as hard I could as the cliff edge came shooting towards me. That's when it all went black. Then I saw a light, or rather two lights staring at me against the black. As they came into focus I could read the two words: Game Over. 'Aw, Dad, I beat you again. Want another go?' So I pressed start on the console for round three of Mario Kart.

If only every aspect of life were that easy. Unfortunately, there are many things that do not have such a handy reset button. Much of life is a lot like a tube of toothpaste. It's easy to squeeze the most we can out of it – but once that's been done it's next to impossible to get it back in and we have to live with the consequences of our decisions.

Many of us feel that our lives are out of control and there is no way to get it back the way it is supposed to be, or the way we would really like it to be. If anyone had a right to feel that it was too late, **it was the thief dying on the cross next to Jesus. His life was over.** He had messed everything up. He had been caught, tried, found guilty, sentenced and was in the process of being executed. His dreams of watching his grandchildren skip around his garden while he sat with a cool drink under his vines were never going to come true. All that awaited him was a painful and humiliating end. What hope could he possibly have as his heart was straining beyond repair?

But it is to this man, a condemned thief maybe minutes away from death, that Jesus offers hope of a new life. If it wasn't too late for him then perhaps it's not too late for any of us.

A last request

Apparently, just before he died, poet and playwright Oscar Wilde said, with characteristic wit: 'Either this wallpaper goes or I do.' His last request was for a change of scenery and I guess he got his wish. For the criminal dying next to Jesus, his last request has also been recorded: 'Jesus, remember me when you come into your kingdom.'

This was a bizarre request. It was strange for four reasons: because of who was asking, because of whom he was asking, because of what he was asking, and because of when he was asking.

Who?

We have already seen that the man with the last request was no Oscar Wilde.

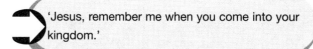

'Jesus, remember me when you come into your kingdom.'

He had contributed less than nothing to society and was dying in blatant disgrace on a public hillside known creepily as 'the Skull'. The request is strange because this thief had no right to ask any favours of anyone – and he knew it.

Perhaps he knew of Jesus' reputation for compassion, forgiveness and justice. Perhaps he knew he had nothing to lose. Nevertheless, he did not bring his request to Jesus with excuses, reasons or arguments. He doesn't say, 'Remember me because I did the best I could in the circumstances,' nor 'Remember me because I managed to do a little bit more good in my life than bad,' nor 'Remember me because I had a tough upbringing and it wasn't my fault,' nor even, 'Remember me because I did what I thought was right.'

This criminal does not appeal to anything he has done in order to be remembered by Jesus. In fact, he has already confessed to being guilty as charged. By asking Jesus to remember him he is asking for mercy. He wants Jesus to accept him, not because of anything he has done, but *despite* everything he has done. He wants Jesus to accept him, *because* of what Jesus was doing for him.

Whom?

The second reason this request is strange is because of the person to whom it was made: King Jesus. Strange, because Jesus could not have looked less like a king. He was hanging on a cross, not sitting on a throne. He was naked, not clothed in royal robes. He was alone, not surrounded by his armies and servants. On his head was a crown of thorns not a crown of gold. He was dying in public humiliation, writhing in agony and covered in blood, sweat and tears.

It would have been easy to go with the flow. Go with the sea of public opinion. Go with the picture in front of him. But the thief saw what nobody else saw. He glimpsed at the last moment a life beyond the grave, where he would have to give account. And right beside him was a man who claimed to be sent from God, not recognized as king on earth, but also about to enter the afterlife. Suddenly, it was as clear as day for the thief: Jesus was more than a good man or a wise religious teacher – they didn't get crucified anyway. Jesus was king of the next life. Who better to turn to for mercy?

What?

The third reason the request is strange is because of what he is requesting. The thief is asking for a relationship with Jesus after death.

I have to admit I can't get very excited about kings and queens or Buckingham Palace, Shmuckingham Palace. The idea that descendants of a random family line get to be rich and powerful, however dysfunctional, is hardly democratic. And all that show of hand waving, small dogs, hats and a speech interrupting my Christmas Day siesta just does not wave my flag.

The poor thief didn't have any better associations. He may have associated kingship with the almighty Caesar, living halfway around the known world, and sending his armies to conquer, crush and control places like Israel. Or he may have associated kingship with the brutality of Herod's family, with its public scandal and murder plots.

Either way, the thief did not seem to have a problem calling Jesus a king. But Jesus as we have seen is not a typical king. He does not use power for personal gain nor does he force our allegiance. He created and cared for the universe, but lived amongst the poor and excluded. He healed, helped and honoured people, but also accepted taunts, suffering and pain at the hands of people.

The way Jesus chose to live and die in humility can make it difficult to recognize Jesus as king. Partly, we have very different ideas of kingship. Partly, we are very focused on the here and now, the ups and downs of life in our own small corner of the world. Partly, we are just very busy ruling our own lives. I make coffee to suit myself, with the right type and amount of milk. I listen to whatever music I like, at the volume I choose, wherever and whenever I fancy.

I wear the clothes I like, choose the holidays that suit me, and pick friends I get along with. **Most of my life I spend as though I myself were the centre of the universe.**

Becoming a Christian is recognizing a relationship with Jesus, not as our own spiritual butler but as our king. This is what the thief does when he finally realizes he has made a complete mess of running his life himself.

When?

Of course, the thief did not have very much of his life on earth left to live under Jesus' authority, but the moments that were left were certainly important ones. For most of us, following the thief's example, and putting ourselves under Jesus' authority, has huge implications for how we are going to spend the rest of our lives.

Many people imagine Christianity to be a bolt-on addition to life. Christians often appear to live in the same way as everyone else, but with a few extra things like going to church services, reading the Bible and praying a bit more. However, the shift that takes place when someone decides to become a Christian is much more radical.

(Luke 3:11–14)

Firstly, if Jesus is our king then our first priority is to live to please him, honouring him with everything – not just with the time that's left over after we have done the things we want. Jesus' life gives us a model for how to do that. The way he treated people, his compassion, his integrity and his justice become the model for our lives.

Secondly, if Jesus is our king there will be change. There will be ways we have been living that are no longer appropriate. Living to please ourselves is not an option. Ignoring and disobeying God is not fitting. Turning away from self-centred living is called repentance. Most people think repentance is about not doing bad things, but Jesus' cousin, John, painted a bigger picture

"The man with two tunics should share with him who has none, and the one who has food should do the same."

Tax collectors also came to be baptised. "Teacher," they asked, "what should we do?"

"Don't collect any more than you are required to," he told them.

Then some soldiers asked him, "And what should we do?"

He replied, "Don't extort money and don't accuse people falsely—be content with your pay."

Becoming a Christian does not mean we throw away all our possessions, but we learn to share them. Becoming a Christian does not necessarily mean that we change our jobs, but it may mean we change the way we do them. Becoming a Christian does not mean just being better on the outside, but it affects our internal motivations too. We are not expected to become monks, dump friendships, go all religious or become freaks. However, it does have a significant impact on every area of our life. This needs to be carefully considered.

Whenever we are ready for this sort of commitment, it is never too late. It may seem a huge step, but compared to the steps Jesus took to save our life, nothing is too much if we are trying to express to him our gratitude. When we pray, 'Thank you for what Jesus did for me on the cross' the words should correspond to a lifetime of grateful living.

Whenever we are ready for this sort of commitment, it is **never too late.**

4: 'It's too soon . . .'

Some would call it living on the edge. Some would call it adrenaline-seeking. Some would call it sheer laziness. The yellow light on my dashboard is nearly always flashing, and many a journey has been spent in panic looking for a petrol station where I can fill up. I know I should check and top up regularly at the services around the corner from my house, but it's one of those tiresome jobs I just can't be bothered to schedule in. Unfortunately, my tendency to put petrol to the back of my mind could get me into a lot of trouble. One day I am going to strand my family of six on the hard shoulder of the motorway in the freezing rain because I live in a dream world where I can just keep driving forever.

Many of us live our lives the way I drive my car. We think we have all the time in the world and that we can just keep running forever. But avoiding thinking about the end of our days is as crazy as trying to avoid filling up the car.

You could take your cue from my driving tactics and wait until the last minute when the warning signs start flashing. You could take your cue from the story of the thief on the cross and wait right until the final moment before you ask God to sort out the mess that is your life. While it is true that it is never too late to turn to Jesus, it is also true that it is never too soon.

Graham Greene's classic novel *Brighton Rock* tells of a gangster who believes he can do all the evil he wants and then repent on his deathbed. The problem is that his death comes suddenly. He has acid thrown in his face and falls off a cliff before he has a chance to say any last words to God. Since none of us knows how or when our lives will come to an end, it is prudent to think seriously about these things while we can. Being a Christian is more than fire insurance, a get-out-of-hell-free card or a pass to Paradise City. Let's see why.

The thief on the cross has just spoken his last words: that strange request to be remembered by Jesus when he inherits his kingdom. Now the innocent man hanging alongside the thief also speaks out. His words were not curses called down on the self-righteous religious rulers, the sarcastic soldiers or the cocksure criminal. His words were not a complaint at the injustice, a threat of vengeance or a request for pain relief. No, he chose to speak words of great comfort and hope to the repentant reprobate beside him. This is so typical of Jesus. In the midst of all the inhumanity, suffering and bloodshed, Jesus' words offered real hope to a morally bankrupt man close to death.

Jesus makes him a promise that has helped millions of people around the world: 'I tell you the truth, today you will be with me in paradise.' This calls for a closer look.

The promise is guaranteed

 'I tell you the truth, today you will be with me in Paradise.'

Jesus used a well-known idiom, 'I tell you the truth', which indicates what he was offering was not a vague or casual hope, but a definite promise. Jesus wanted the thief to be in no doubt that he was offering him a guaranteed place in paradise.

People around the world have recorded a wide variety of impressions of paradise in literature and art. Some see it as a garden, others as a city. Some see clouds, angels and harps; others see friends, family and pets. Jesus, however, only describes paradise as being 'with me'. The important thing about life after death is that life in relationship with God is the highlight of eternity.

If we spend our lives rejecting God, then he will not force us to be with him for eternity, but will grant us the independence we have always sought. The trouble is, everything we know as good is a gift from God, whether we recognize it or not, so our choice to reject God leads us to an eternal destiny – in the God-forsaken place the Bible calls hell.

This account shows that there is another option. Most people that day chose to reject Jesus, but one man chose to respect him. This is the choice we are faced with and it is a serious choice as it affects where we spend eternity – with God in paradise, or apart from him in hell.

The promise is immediate

Jesus is able to tell the thief that on the very day of his death he would be in paradise. This would have been a huge surprise to those listening. Many Jewish people believed the afterlife would begin on the last day of history. Jesus challenged this with these words and an event that took place three days later.

After Jesus was pronounced dead by the Roman soldiers, his body was released and prepared for burial, and then placed in a borrowed sealed tomb, outside which a Roman guard was posted to ward off body snatchers. The disciples went into hiding for fear of being arrested. Yet three days later, they are not only back out in public, but fearlessly declaring that Jesus is alive, explaining to all around that they saw him, touched him and had breakfast with him.

The resurrection of Jesus from the dead is the reason why Christianity didn't end at the crucifixion. It demonstrates the truthfulness of Jesus' teaching and the effectiveness of his sacrificial death on the cross. Also, it offers a hope of resurrection for anyone who dies trusting in him.

The thief certainly did not have time to get into a discussion on the theology of the afterlife – the whens and the hows. The important thing was that the promised and surprising immediacy of paradise would have brought him incredible hope, as he endured the worst pain imaginable. He only had to hang in there a short while longer.

The promise is comforting

This man was experiencing the throes of a long, slow and painful demise. After the crowd had enjoyed the spectacle of torture for a few hours, the soldiers would speed up the grand finale by breaking the thief's legs, so that he would not be able to use his lower body muscles to push up to exhale. Then, the crowd would watch as he died, from either suffocation or his heart giving out.

We might feel a comforting promise under these circumstances would be one which offered immediate release, or unmitigated joy. Many people expect becoming a Christian to involve a rush of emotion, and immediate miraculous deliverance from all their problems. But the promise Jesus gave did not suddenly transport the thief out of his circumstances, dreadful though they were. However, this did not mean the promise was invalid, or void of sympathy. Jesus was not sitting on a sofa on the sidelines, spouting empty 'you'll be fine' platitudes. He was suffering alongside and his words had weight that really helped.

Some people experience God's miraculous intervention in their life when they become a Christian. But many don't. Although we believe God has the power to change any situation, he often chooses not to. In this case, the thief was the only one that day who, instead of demanding Jesus show his power by saving himself, or insisting Jesus save him from his terrible circumstances, humbly requested that Jesus remembered him. But, in those circumstances, Jesus saved his life with the promise of something far more precious: peace with God.

As it became harder to breathe, the thief knew Jesus' promise was getting closer. His suffering was temporary, and his hope was eternal. Jesus' words were something to cling to through the physical pain, through the jeers of the crowd and the bitter words of the soldiers. Jesus' promise has brought comfort to many men and women who have died in similar circumstances in the Roman Colosseum, the Nazi torture chambers, the Cambodian killing fields or in modern-day prisons in places like Sudan, North Korea or Indonesia where Christians are still persecuted.

The promise is for us

The majority of us are not facing the imminent threat of death. Nevertheless, we do not know when our end will come. Even if we did, we may get round to cleaning up the house and sorting out our finances, but it would be impossible to clean up our act, or sort out our lives by ourselves. Jesus accepts us in the mess we are in and it is never too soon to know the assurance of being prepared.

Secondly, the promise affects not only how we die, but how we live. Jesus' promise to be with us stands this side of paradise. By asking him to take control of our life, and having him involved, the rest of our days will never be the same.

A little hope goes a long way. We know this as we part with our cash for a lottery ticket each weekend. We know this as we book a holiday, plan a party or save up for a treat. Hope for life beyond the grave can transform the way we live now.

Many people who say that it is too soon to become a Christian are operating under the assumption that becoming a follower of Jesus is to be put off until the last possible minute, because God is a cosmic spoilsport. If we can have all the fun we want, and then sneak in at the last minute, we can beat the system – we can have our cake and eat it.

Let's go back to the driving analogy. We want to drive our own cars until they are trashed, and only then will we let another driver come in and drive it to the scrapyard. On the other hand, I learned something on a go-karting day with mates. I loved driving the kart – it felt so low to the ground and the acceleration took my breath away. At the end of the day a professional driver took us around the track on a special two-seater kart. I was no bad passenger on that occasion: it felt like I was strapped to a rocket as we went full pelt sailing round the bends. He made my shabby attempts at racing look like a toddler in a pedal car. He got so much more out of the kart than I ever could or would. Suddenly, being a passenger was taken to a whole new level.

This experience helped me to reconsider what it means to have Jesus right at the core of our lives, not as a cosmic spoilsport, but as the cosmic champion. Not turning us into drones following his every command, but releasing the full potential of our lives, skills and passions. **Not simply by providing us with a manual, but by empowering us and transforming us with his Holy Spirit.** It is never too soon to start finding out where that will take us by deciding: 'I want to live for you.'

Hope for life beyond the grave can **transform** the way we live now.

Conclusion: How to be saved

So we have seen from the last words of a dying thief that any of us can be saved if we are willing to respect God's authority, realize our own failings, reach out to Jesus for forgiveness and then recognize him as our rightful leader – a leader who loves us enough to die for us and can be trusted to know how we can best live.

'I'm too good . . .'

When we measure ourselves up against other people we can appear fine. But when we compare ourselves with Jesus we realize how far we have fallen short. If we face up to the fact that we will have to come face to face with God, we should approach him respectfully, to make peace with the Creator of the universe while we have the chance.

Lord God . . .

'I'm too bad . . .'

It doesn't take very long for many of us to realize we haven't lived as we should have or could have. The story of the thief on the cross tells us no matter what we have done, if we admit our failings and ask for forgiveness, there is hope for us. Jesus' specialist subject seems to be compassion and forgiveness to broken people who ask for help.

Forgive me for what I have done . . .

'It's too late . . .'

If a man can find forgiveness in the middle of his execution, then there is hope for all of us, however late we have left it. This is possible not because of anything we have done to deserve it, but because of what Jesus did to make it possible. He took the fall on our behalf, so that we don't have to pay the heavy price of punishment but can have another chance to live for God.

Thank you for what Jesus did for me on the cross . . .

'It's too soon . . .'

Death and eternity seem an awfully long way ahead to most of us. We don't like to think about them. But Jesus offers us a promise that is good for this life and the next. His promise transforms the way we live and the way we die.

I want to live for you . . .

'Amen' is a traditional way to end a prayer. It means, 'I have thought this through carefully and I mean it sincerely.' If you agree with all these words, it may be time for you to say them not to yourself or to the book, but to God himself. Perhaps use the words as a framework to articulate what you really want to say to God about your own life in your own words. The moment you turn to talk to God a relationship begins that can save your life.

Amen.